A PERSONAL MISSION STATEMENT

YOUR ROAD MAP TO HAPPINESS

BY MICHAL STAWICKI

www.expandbeyondyourself.com

September 2014
Copyright © 2014 Michal Stawicki
All rights reserved worldwide.
ISBN: 1508505969
ISBN-13: 978-1508505969

Table of Contents

Introduction

This book is intended to save a lot of your time. When you want to make a mission statement, you usually browse the Web looking for clues, samples and helpful tips. This is all new to you and you want to understand the concept better and find some guidance. Going through a heap of garbage info. is unavoidable. And that's the beauty of my manual - you don't need to employ Google any more. Everything you need to create a personal mission statement is here. What is more, the questions and mental exercises included in the book are compilations from more than a dozen personal development books I've read and courses I've taken: "The 7 Habits of Highly Effective People," "Cultivating an Unshakable Character," "The Slight Edge," to name just a few. The pushy marketer would say, "You don't need to purchase them to gain the knowledge, so you save at least $100 by buying this little book."

I share with you what my personal mission statement creation process looked like. In that example,

I show you which points I consider vital in the creation of a mission statement in general.

When I get personal and all "about me," I change the font style. I hope my story will give you additional insights into the creation process. If my personal ruminations and comments don't interest you, skip those parts - you still will be able to create a mission statement. You will find a full story of my creation process in Chapter 7. I give you there also a peek into my personal mission statement.

I've written my mission statement inspired by Stephen R. Covey's book "The 7 Habits of Highly Effective People." It is not necessary to read it in order to create your personal mission statement, but it surely won't hurt if you do.

What is a Personal Mission Statement and why is it So Important?

"You can, you should, and if you're brave enough to start, you will."

— Stephen King

In his audio program, "Cultivating an Unshakable Character," Jim Rohn said that the natural order of things is to chisel your character first and the success comes from your character. To chisel your inner self, you first need to know yourself. I think a personal mission statement is the best road map to build your character and consequently your success, however you define it.

A personal mission statement is your philosophy, your creed. "It focuses on what you want to be (character) and what you want to do (contributions and achievements), and on the values or principles upon which being and doing are based."[1] It is supposed to allow you to state your own constitution based on your deepest values, so you can lead life premised on them.

In other words, you state your purpose for being here. Not me. Not your parents. Not your kids. Not

---

[1] "The 7 Habits of the Highly Effective People", Stephen R. Covey

your siblings, friends, enemies; not your boss or co-workers. You.

A personal mission statement is about your life's purpose. This purpose determines the quality and quantity of your life. Literally.

There are scientific bases to the sentences above. If you are interested, please familiarize yourself with Logotherapy. Its creator - Victor Frankl - based his research on his own experiences in a death camp during World War II. Putting his work in a few simple words - people who realize their life's purpose can survive, whereas people without it die. This conclusion is drawn upon the extreme circumstances of death camp, but it is true in ordinary circumstances, as well. People who know what they live for tend to have happier and more fulfilling lives than those who don't.

Victor Frankl was convinced that every human being has his/her unique life's purpose. Maybe you even agree with that statement. But it's not enough to know it exists. To have the vague feeling of your mission. What you need is a concrete purpose. You need to know by heart the exact words which will guide you through everyday decisions. Thus, you need a personal mission statement.

Life's purpose - it sounds grandiloquent, doesn't it? But it doesn't have to be lofty, enormous. Most of us are just common folks who struggle with our fears, doubts, anxieties, past. We don't dream of being a hero, rescuing the world. We dream about a few sources of income to be able to support our families and look to the future with hope. To heal our relationships. To break up our addictions. To reduce the pile of our problems.

Not everybody is a CEO, a best-selling author, a brilliant inventor or doctor. Teachers, housewives, clerks, programmers, grandfathers and nurses have their purpose in life, too. It just has a different scale. And who knows? Maybe in following your personal mission statement, you will grow beyond your wildest dreams.

We dealt with the "mission statement" part of the expression. But I think that the best part of it is "personal." It is your creation; your work from the bottom of your heart. It is not given, not imposed from outside. It is something that you, personally, came up with considering your destiny.

Affirmations are good, but a personal mission statement is better. Those are your words, describing your mission, your life purpose. You have no internal reservations listening to them, repeating them. They will never be boring or unmeaningful to you. You will never be tired of them.

I made my personal mission statement at the beginning of November 2012. I meditate upon it every day. I recorded it and I listen to it almost every day - usually several times a day - while doing shopping, cleaning, making meals, commuting.

And it works.

I'm doing things I had never done before. For example, I had never written a book before. I'm thinking and acting in a way I didn't before. And, from time to time, when facing a tough decision, I hear the words of my personal mission statement in my head. It is a gradual process. It's not a magic wand. I'm still far, far away from realizing my full potential. It will not materialize within days, weeks or even years. But thanks to my personal mission statement, I'm closer to it every day. If you can't say the same, I strongly urge you to take some time, read this book from cover to cover, question yourself and actually do as many mental exercises as necessary to hammer out and state in writing your life's purpose.

Bronie Ware worked for many years in palliative care, caring for patients in the last 12 weeks of their lives. She found the five most common regrets of dying people[2] are:

1. I wish I'd had the courage to live a life true to myself, not the life others expected of me.
2. I wish I didn't work so hard.
3. I wish I'd had the courage to express my feelings.
4. I wish I had stayed in touch with my friends.
5. I wish that I had let myself be happier.

Creating a personal mission statement seems to be a good starting point to avoid such regrets at the end of your life. Having it, all you have to do is to simply follow it. It doesn't matter if you just emerged from adolescence or are on a deathbed. Just do it.

---

2 http://www.inspirationandchai.com/Regrets-of-the-Dying.html

Discover Your Mission

"The meaning of our existence is not invented by ourselves, but rather detected."

-Viktor E. Frankl, *Man's Search for Meaning*

My short recipe for making a personal mission statement is: examine yourself to the verge of insanity; use imagination; write everything down.

A personal mission statement is personal. Every single one is unique. Wally Amos' has just one sentence. Mine has about 1,300 words. There is no "right" way to do it. There is only your way. Everything is up to you. The pace, the final form, how, when and where you will create it.

You don't need to hurry while making your personal mission statement. It doesn't have to be perfect or beautiful, short or long. It has to be YOURS. I was struggling for more than a month creating mine. Wally Amos hammered out his own during a single flight to Hawaii. I suppose it has a lot to do with him already being a person focused on his life purpose. And a lot to do with me not thinking for long years about where my life was headed.

The first step is to decide that you are going to create your mission statement, period. Put it on your to-do list, promise yourself you will do it, give yourself a deadline, put a task in your calendar - do whatever you do when you are serious about finishing something. I advise you to work daily on your personal mission statement. Block some time and stick to it. If you have no time - wake up 15 minutes earlier every day. Make a temporal habit out of it, just for the statement creation time. In my experience, that's how things get done.

a. Examine yourself

"Self-analysis may disclose weaknesses which one does not like to acknowledge. This form of examination is essential to all who demand of Life more than mediocrity and poverty. Remember, as you check yourself point by point, that you are both the court and the jury, the prosecuting attorney and the attorney for the defense, and that you are the plaintiff and the defendant, also, that you are on trial. Face the facts squarely. Ask yourself definite questions and demand direct replies. When the examination is over, you will know more about yourself. (...) You are after the truth. Get it, no matter at what cost even though it may temporarily embarrass you!" - Napoleon Hill, "Think and Grow Rich"

I don't know how it is with you, but I don't like self-analyzing. I was able to avoid it for about 16 years. However, working on my personal mission statement, I decided it is so important that I included such a sentence in it:

"To know myself is the most powerful and - in the end - the only weapon I have."

Get used to questioning yourself. Prepare internally for coming back to the moments of greatest pain and greatest joy in your life. For actually living through them once again in your mind. Please do not dwell on painful details for too long. Those questions about your past are meant to give you the knowledge about you, not to just bring back tragic events and make you miserable. Always have the end goal in your mind. You are looking for your destiny. That's your ultimate focus.

*I haven't had many dark moments in my past, but there are a few. I don't like to recall them. I don't like to think about them. Heck, I don't even like **me** when I'm belaboring them. The experience of going through them once again was only slightly more bearable by doing it with the purpose of improving my life. It was also made slightly more bearable by virtue of being detached from those moments by time and distance. Doesn't sound inviting, does it? However, there is enormous healing potential in facing such painful, past events.*

My experience is that the fear of thinking about them is greater than the terror of those dark moments themselves. The past is past; it's nothing real. It's just a memory in my mind - images, sounds and feelings. I can freeze them and tweak them the way I wish.

I propose a lot of questions and mental exercises in this chapter. You don't have to answer and do them all. But how many? As many as necessary to create your personal mission statement. And remember: nobody can substitute for you; you are the only person in the whole universe who can do this job. But I can help you.

Below, I give you a list of questions and simple tasks. Answer as many of them as you wish, in any succession you find comfortable. If you come up with any other questions, if one answer leads you to a new question, don't hesitate to include them in your creation process. Whatever questions you choose to answer - write like crazy. Writing it down is a very important, crucial part of creating your personal mission statement.

I have about 5-8 pages of raw material handwritten from the creation process.

1. Identify the most important roles you perform or you want to perform in the future.

   For me they were: father, husband, son, brother, church community member, employee, friend, writer.

2. What are the three most important values, qualities, factors in your life?

3. Who do you want to become?

   Well, if you know the answers to the questions 2 and 3 you are halfway through your personal mission statement. It's not so easy to answer them just out of the blue. You don't know? - don't worry, just go through the rest of questions.

4. What do you want to do?
5. What do you want to see?
6. What do you want to have?
7. Where do you want to go?

List those goals/wishes without limits in your mind - as everything is possible. Work on them till your mind is emptied. Stop when you cannot think about anything new. Then take each item from the list and ask yourself: Why? Why would I want it? What's a deep reason?

8. What is the meaning of your everyday work?
9. What do others think of you? What are the most surprising opinions you heard about you? How did those opinions surprise you? What can you discover about yourself from those surprising areas?
10. What do you like to do? What is your passion? What are your hobbies?
11. What have you been doing for the years? What does this tell you about yourself?

That one is my original. I didn't find it in any book I had read. People today are constantly looking for something new. This game now; that one next month. This cereal today; another next year. This social media now; completely different next year. And we are overlooking what is constant in our lives. You don't wonder about attending your church for years; about being involved in local community issues; about going to the gym every Saturday; reading one book every week. It's just something you have always been doing. However, it can (and usually does) mean something significant about you.

12. What did you like to do when you were a kid?

13. As a child, who or what did you want to be when you grew up?

This particular question didn't help me much, in itself. I didn't get an illumination: "The dentist! I wanted to be a dentist! Teeth is my destiny!" Nope. Being a child, I wanted to be a farmer or a forester. What it really gave me were the leads to other ruminations. I wanted to be a farmer, because I admired my grandfather who was a farmer. I wanted to be a forester, because in a wilderness, it's easy for me to feel I'm close to God.

14. What are you good at? Why?
15. What do you like doing? What activity and/or work do you find interesting and/or challenging?
16. What activities are you trying to avoid? Why?
17. What do you consider your greatest failure? Why?
18. What do you consider your greatest success? Why? Was it hard to choose this one? Can you think of more success examples?
19. What are the three greatest achievements in your career? What are the three greatest achievements in your career as recognized by your superiors? Are they different from those pointed out by you? Why is that so?

I know, it sounds like you are on an interview. But in a way it is. And you are the one who is hiring yourself for the biggest job in your life. On interviews, I always feel like I need to answer in a way that pleases my potential employer. When you are on both sides of the interview, you can be 100 percent honest.

20. Who are the most important people in your life? Why? What do you admire in them?
21. What sort of activity or work gives you the greatest feeling of importance and personal satisfaction?
22. What have you always wanted to do but been afraid to attempt?
23. What one great thing would you dare to dream if you knew you could not fail?
24. Remind yourself of three recent situations where you felt stressed. What made you feel that way? How did you act in those situations? How would you like to act in similar cases in the future? Imagine a specific situation and yourself acting in this new, improved way.
25. Remind yourself of three recent situations where you felt loved or happy. What made you feel that way? What can you do to repeat such situations more often?
26. List your life's goals. Imagine you have no limitations. That you are like Nick Vujicic or Anthony Robbins. Imagine then, that you could be absolutely guaranteed of success in any of your goals. Which one goal would you choose to achieve? Why this one?
27. Recall the works, jobs, projects you enjoyed doing. Why? Name the specific factors which caused you to enjoy them.

Several years ago I worked on a very big, serious project. I was stressed out of my mind. I labored like never before. And I enjoyed it - mostly. I felt my input was of the utmost importance. I was never short of problems to resolve. On my shoulders rested big responsibility for a few core systems' functionality.

I identified my factors: importance, troubleshooting, responsibility and the sense of growth.

b. Imaginative tasks

"Expand your mind. Visualize in rich detail. Involve as many emotions and feelings as possible. Involve as many of the senses as you can." - Stephen R. Covey, *The 7 Habits of the Highly Effective People*

"Imagination is everything. It is the preview of life's coming attractions." - Albert Einstein

You are looking for your purpose in life. Listen to your heart. Deep soul-searching connotes with seclusion, peace and quiet. And rightly so. The ideal situation would be if you could go for two weeks of vacation to meditate about your destiny. However, the world is not ideal. Don't allow it to scuttle your personal mission statement creation.

I have not had many times of seclusion, peace and quiet in my life. As a full time employee, father of three and husband, I have few opportunities to find even an hour of silence. The only two days in a year I'm away from my family are when I go for a retreat with my church community. This is my time of peace and calmness. Coincidently (if you believe in coincidences), the retreat had been scheduled into 2/3 of the period during which I had been working on my personal mission statement. And, yes, the understanding of my purpose came at the retreat. But serenity alone was not enough to finish it. I still needed two more weeks to make it ready to use.

Necessary elements for your mental exercises are: your mind and something to write with (pen and paper, smartphone, tablet, PDA, PC). Think about your daily schedule and find the periods when those elements are available.

Hint: when you watch TV, your mind is not quite there.

I am "blessed" with a job to which I commute for over an hour in one direction. In the case of my personal mission statement creation effort, it was really a blessing. I did most of my mental exercises on a train, on the way back from work, with loud music in my earphones separating me from the conversations of co-passengers. Writing things down while riding on a train was a challenge.

On top of all the questioning and mental exercises, I encourage you to give some more time to the activities you normally use as a means to reach inside your soul and mind. Study your important lecture. I don't know what's important for you - it can be your diary, the Bible, personal development book which influenced you most, letters from your spouse or parents, favorite poem. Pray, meditate, talk with your spouse or friends.

All those different challenges might seem a little scary at first, but I assure you they are also fun. You can get to know yourself from a totally unexpected angle.

I loved to play strategic - card and computer - games. While looking for my life purpose, I realized through a few different mental tasks that I love to play games because I love excellence. Getting better every game, beating records, comparing my results with peers - it all sums up to the feeling that I'm progressing, moving forward. It was the surrogate for achievement in my life.

1. Visualize the relationship in your marriage after 20 and then after 40 years. Try to capture its essence created over a period of that many years.
2. Imagine that you have only six months of life left. How would it change your actions? Mr. Covey invited his students to play this game of mind for a week and keep a diary of their experiences.
3. Recall the time of biggest suffering in your life. Examine it in your mind and ask yourself questions. What caused the suffering? What got you through that experience? How did you act? How would you like to act if something like that ever happened again? Imagine such a situation in the future and yourself acting in this new, improved way.
4. Recall the time when you felt most loved. Why did you feel loved then? What can you do to attract similar experiences in the future?
5. Visualize the end of your present career. Will it be a retirement? Will you change your occupation? What contributions, what

achievements will you want to have made in your field?

6. What would you do – how would you change your life – if you received $1,000,000 cash today? Imagine a situation that is comprehensible to you - winning a lottery, being given an inheritance, getting an enormous order for your business. Put yourself in your mind in front of such a pile of cash and see - in your mind - how would that change your life?

7. Write down at least three turning points in your life. They can be negative or positive - death in the family, getting married, change of job, birth of your first child, severe illness, going to a college - whatever made a significant change in your life. How did those events impact you? Why? Try to think of someone, who in similar circumstances changed his or her life in exactly the opposite direction. If you don't know such a person, try to search in the Internet - there is an experience of all humanity preserved. As unique as each of us is, you can probably find such a story. Then dwell on the differences between you and them. Why did you choose to act your way, whereas there was an alternative? Did you act according to your values or against them?

8. Visualize how your life will be in five, 10 and 20 years from now, if you don't make any significant decisions for all those years. Imagine you let your life "go with the flow." Dwell on your finances, health, relationships, personal growth,

spirituality, career. Do you really want your life to look like this? What is missing in those pictures? Think more in terms of values and feelings than of physical possessions.

If you answered: "Yes, I like my life that way. Nothing is missing", then you already live your personal mission. To make a statement, you need just to write down what are you doing now.

9. There is an NLP technique called "the core transformation." It is supposed to help in finding motivation for achieving your goals, but I found it very helpful in expanding my vision. Start from any goal. Write it down. And I mean any goal. The more significant, the quicker you will go through the exercise, but you can even pick something from your daily to-do list.

   Imagine you have achieved your goal definitively and absolutely. What does this achievement give you, which is even more wonderful than your goal?

   And again, what does it give you?

   For example, your goal is to earn $100,000 a year. Imagine you are earning this sum – what does it give you, which is even more wonderful than the $100,000?

   Your answer: I can quit my job and spend more time with my family.

Imagine you quit your job and spend more time with your family. What does it give you, which is even more wonderful than that?

Your answer: Well, I can help my friends now, take care of their kids when they are at work, organize sport tournaments for kids.

Imagine you help your friends taking care of their kids and organize sports tournaments for kids. What does it give you, which is even more wonderful?

Your answer: the whole neighborhood is a happier place right now. Our kids are healthier. We have more engaging events. People come from all over the country to participate in tournaments. Other districts start to imitate us.

And so on, and so on. The string of questions leads you to the point, where the world is really perfect. Nothing can give you an "even more wonderful experience."

Two reminders: Imagine, means really imagine. Try to see the outcome of every question in your mind. And write down every answer!

I did that exercise on a train on my way home from work. So I think (as with any activity) the only bad way to do it, is not to do it at all. Any other way is a good one ;)

10. Visualize your own funeral. Who is there? What are they saying about you – your family, friends, church members, work mates? Write your own specific eulogy. Actually write it out.

If you want audio or Kindle version of this book, go to:

http://ExpandBeyondYourself.com/pms/

Chiseling Your Personal Mission Statement out of Raw Material

"It is the nature of man to rise to greatness if greatness is expected of him."

- John Steinbeck, author

After going through all those questions and stretching your mind by all those mental exercises, you hopefully gathered a lot of material in the form of notes. You should now have at least vague feelings of what your life is about and how you see your personal mission statement. Well, that was the purpose of preceding chapters. At this stage of my work, I had quite vivid ideas about both. Also, my friends with whom I shared a much less detailed version of the creation manual were able to make their mission statements, so I assume it's the natural order of things.

Having a multitude of answers and visions written down, creating your personal mission statement should be reduced to skim and trim of the raw material. Don't hesitate to cut out any non-essentials. The ultimate purpose of your personal mission statement is to constantly have in mind all the most important areas of your life. While making decisions of what to leave in and what to throw out your leading question is:

Do I really want to think about it every day for the rest of my life?

Let this question wander at the back of your mind while phrasing the mission statement. I encourage you to make your statement as condensed as possible. I eventually knew mine by heart, but it took me a few months to imprint those 1,300 words into my mind. I'm sure Wally Amos had much less trouble with remembering his one-sentence-long statement. Examples included in "The 7 Habits of the Highly Effective People" book were 200-300 words long.

On the other hand, you don't want to focus on one or two areas and neglect everything else. Providing for your family is important, but what's the use of all money in the world, if you have no time to spend with your relatives? What to choose? What to cut out? Do you remember the "personal" part? You are the judge. It's your life; it's all up to you.

I suppose my statement is so expanded, because I've been neglecting my inner life for so many years. No goal settings, no thinking about the future (except for occasionally worrying to insanity), shallow prayers, shallow interactions with other people. That all summed up so many areas desperately crying out for improvement WHEN I started to think about my life seriously. Thus, I recognized more than a dozen that I needed to work on and they are rarely described by a single sentence.

OK, so you have your notes. What else can you use? Whatever your imagination finds appropriate. Fragments of books. Quotes of famous people. Fragments of letters or love poems you've written/received. Your favorite song's text. Holy Book of your religion. Commercial slogans ("Just do it!").

Almost 60 percent of my statement are the Bible's fragments and other books' quotes in proportion 10 to one. The rest consists of my 'free' thoughts.

Mr. Covey advised to write the personal mission statement as a list of affirmations: in present tense, positive, personal, emotional and visual. And, by visual, he meant something easy to imagine. He used an example of imagining your child misbehaving and your improved response full of wisdom, love and self-control.

In his book, I also found an example of a mission statement in the future tense: "I'll this; I'll that." I also came across some samples on the Internet, where negative statements were used: "I don't this; I don't that." However, Brian Tracy says that, for some reason, the subconscious mind just ignores negative statements and focuses on positive ones. And personal. And in the present tense. So, if I were you, I would act on both gentlemen's expertise. But still the rule number one is: it's all up to you.

I have already been using my mission statement for six months. I have "don'ts" in two areas -language and procrastination. It's hard to say for sure, but I have the feeling they are weaker than positive affirmations, that their impact is limited. The example of procrastination is an interesting one. I listed specific activities I no longer should be involved in:

- I don't watch TV
- I don't play computer games
- I don't follow the news stream

And I really don't do them or I restricted them enormously. But I found other ways to "kill my time" - checking stats on my blog several times a day, looking for a word of encouragement from my friends on Facebook and on a few specific community's websites, checking my email box - each of them several times a day, which adds up to long, wasted hours.

If you went honestly through chapter 4, you've already questioned yourself to the verge of insanity. Now that you have the answers, the only thing remaining is to arrange them neatly in the form of a personal mission statement. Write down a list of issues you need to focus on. Here is an outline based on the statement of a woman seeking to balance family and work:

- balance
- home
- participation in democratic processes
- children
- self-esteem
- habits
- money management

I found as many as 14 areas which needed to be addressed. They are of such importance to me, that I have to think of them in an appropriate way every day of my life:

- *Love*
- *Children*
- *Wife*
- *Gratitude*
- *Failure*
- *Achievement*
- *Wealth*
- *Giving*
- *Motivation*
- *Following my friends' examples*
- *Being present - focus on Now*
- *Self-examination*
- *Language*
- *Persistence*

After identifying those issues, all you have to do is to put them into words. The order of subjects in your mission statement can be important, but generally speaking, it isn't. A personal mission statement is built on one's core values, which are all equally important. Your core values are like the car's wheels. The car will not drive without one. Or, they are like body parts. How is an eye better than a hand or leg? They are equally needed.

Composing the final version of my statement, I knew only that I wanted to have Love and Family at the beginning and Persistence at the end. The order of the other topics was more or less random.

Rewriting and rephrasing your mission statement is absolutely normal, expected and even desired. We are talking about your life's constitution. It's not something to take lightly. It is important to express it thoughtfully and carefully. If you are an artistic soul, you may create it in the form of a poem, painting or song. But most of us are down to earth folks, and we need just a couple of straightforward sentences concerning several chosen subjects.

Mr. Covey warned in his book that getting used to a personal mission statement might take a few weeks or months. Don't work on phrasing yours until it is "perfect." Be satisfied with the version that is just "good enough." I assure you that after a dozen readings, you'll know which words, phrases, don't sound exactly right and you'll know how to fix them.

My experience is fully agreeable with his warning. In the first month, I tweaked several sentences - added a word here, cut one out there. In one case, it was just a matter of inserting a comma into a phrase. I've also targeted the whole point which I included solely by following the suggestion of others, not my own heart. The version of the statement I'm using now is good enough, but I already know how to make it better. And I will make it better.

I Have It, What's Next?

"An ounce of action is worth a ton of theory."

- Ralph Waldo Emerson

Your personal mission statement is not a certificate of accomplishment to be put into the drawer. It is supposed to be your lens, starting point, the source of focus. Use it.

Beware of feeling like you're lying when you say the words of your mission statement like: "I help people all over the world to deal with their obesity problem." Stephen King hasn't been an author for all of his life. Anthony Robbins wasn't born a millionaire. Rome wasn't built in a day. If it's your destiny, it is going to happen. It is just a matter of time. And you can always "soften" the message in such a way that it will be 100-percent true: "I'm becoming a person who helps people all over the world ..."

Word of caution: don't expect your personal mission statement to come true within days, weeks or months (unless you designed it in such way - everyone is unique). Remember: it is your mission for the rest of your life, as you see it today. And you don't really mean to end your life within days or months, do you?

The purpose of all the techniques in this chapter is to assimilate your personal mission statement into your life. To soak your mind in it. Which of them you use will depend fully upon your decisions. You may have no time for meditation. No technical skills to create a movie. You may be deaf, so using an audio recording is out of the question. Some people are more susceptible to words, some to sounds, some to images. Choose and build your own strategy in accordance with your occupation, circumstances and temperament.

a) **Read it every day.** Or even better - read it several times a day. If you are more sensible than me, your mission statement is compressed into a few hundred words and reading will take you just a couple of minutes. Create a ritual for it. Compose it into the routine of your day. The best time for this is early morning, when you wake up and/or late evening just before going to sleep.

Always carry your mission statement with you. Skim it once in a while. Read it before making an important decision. Read it before making a minor decision, if it's one which could potentially compromise your values.

b) **Meditate upon it.** It's the same story as with reading - make it a ritual and compose it into your schedule. Take a comfortable position. Clear your mind. Breathe deeply. Let it be just you and the words of the mission statement inside your head.

I really have trouble with the multitude of words in my statement. But they are dear to me, so I won't resign from any part. The simple act of repeating the whole mission statement in my mind, touching particular sentences with my thought, takes me about 20 minutes. It's not a small chunk of time for me - working and commuting consume 12 hours from my day. I often wake up in the middle of the night. I use this time to focus on my mission statement until sleep returns. I fall asleep with its words swirling slowly in my head.

c) Listen to it. Record your personal mission statement and listen to it any time and any place you want - while shopping, jogging, commuting, doing household chores, walking, driving, exercising. You know - when the body works, but the mind is idle.

Nowadays it is ridiculously easy to make your own recording. If your statement is reasonably short you can do it using your cell phone in one short session and there is no need for further editing. If it's a bit longer (like mine ;)) the easiest way to create a recording is to use your computer and free software - for example Audacity.

When recording your personal mission statement, give your best effort to express your deepest emotions through your voice. This way listening to the statement will stir those emotions again and again.

I need five minutes just to read my ample mission statement. It's overly time-consuming, so I came up with the idea of recording. It is 12 minutes long, but I can listen to it several times a day (and I usually do) - on the way from home to the railway station, from the station to the bus stop, from the bus to work, doing shopping, scrubbing the toilet during Saturday's turnout, and in many, many more situations.

d) Visualize it. This is especially important if you included some future aspirations or desired changes in the mission statement. Let's say you procrastinate, but you want to do your job giving your best. So you wrote something like this in your statement: "I fully focus on the current task, so at the end of each day, I feel I've given my best."

Close your eyes. Imagine the situation when you usually procrastinate. Visualize how to avoid the temptation to distract yourself. Imagine yourself committing to 100-percent effort.

You can do similar visualizations with every sentence of your mission statement. It doesn't take a lot of time; you need just a few minutes without external distractions. Such mind exercises will allow you to connect and stay connected to your purpose on an emotional level.

e) Create a vision board. Find pictures and photos corresponding with your mission statement. Stick them to the board. Add some headlines with the words of your mission statement. It's supposed to be put in a visible place where you can see it often.

Visualization is not my strong suit. The images in my mind are colorless, fuzzy, without details. So I think a vision board is a very good idea. I'm gonna do it as an image file on a computer, because I spend most of my time in front of it. I have a slide show in PowerPoint done in 85 percent - I just need to include two more topics. I've gathered all the necessary images and pictures. I plan to finish it within two weeks.

f) Make a mind movie. Its function is similar to a vision board - a mind movie is meant to fire up your imagination. Its main advantage over a vision board is the possibility of adding sound. You can use this advantage twofold - make a movie and add the recording of your personal mission statement as a track or add music dear to your heart. The easiest way to make a mind movie is to create a slide show in PowerPoint or other presentation program. Windows systems include free, simple software also very handy for this purpose - Movie Maker. On Mac, there is iMovie. And there are many free programs on the Internet.

Congratulations and Conclusion

Congratulations. You have done something extraordinary. You have written your personal mission statement. Your own constitution. You have described your purpose, your destiny. You have found your core values. I don't know (yet) how many people did the same. Reportedly only 3 percent of Americans have their goals stated and written down. So I suppose the percentage of those who have their life mission written down is considerably smaller. Welcome to this elite minority. Welcome onto a path to happiness.

I would appreciate you sending me an email with the news that you've made your personal mission statement. I just want to know that my work helped one more person. A simple message "I've written my PMS" to pms@onedollartips.com will be enough, although any other feedback is much welcomed, too. I'm also interested in any unique ways you've come up with to implement your personal mission statement and, of course, in the successes in your life you credit to it.

Live with your personal mission statement, follow it in your daily tasks and one day you will live it.

My Own Personal Mission Statement Creation Process

"I'm becoming a writer."

- Michal, *Personal Mission Statement*

As I said, I had been struggling with my personal mission creation for over one month. And I'm glad I did. Take your time. It's per-so-nal. Some people need time. Some don't. My process of creation looked like this:

– answers to questions from "The 7 Habits ..." book. Visualization tasks listed there

– answers to some more questions from some other personal development books (most of them included in this book)

– some other mental exercises, the most profound was the core transformation technique I included in this book

– visit on Stephen. R. Covey's website; there is a free PMS builder; the only price is an email address. I went through it and gathered more data.

At this step, I had some raw material and the idea for my statement - I was going to use quotes from the Bible extensively. For about 15 years, the Bible study has been the only activity I used to reach within me. For me, it was natural to use it.

Then, I went for a retreat with my church community and I had this blessed time studying the Bible. I wrote down two or three sheets of paper full of quotes and my thoughts wrapped around them.

It took me another week or two to compose my statement. The final version is half the Bible quotes, half my answers-comments to them, organized around 14 topics important to me.

Below are the quotes I used and the way I arranged them. Some of them, I had to find with a specific topic in mind. Some quotes have been with me for years and I created topics around them. The 'abc' letters mean 1st, 2nd or 3rd part of Bible verse. I used the New Jerusalem Bible - a Catholic translation of the Bible published in 1985 - to provide the quotes in English. Here they are:

Introduction (without my comments):

"Let faithful love and constancy never leave you: tie them round your neck, write them on the tablet of your heart. Thus you will find favour and success in the sight of God and of people." Prov. 3: 3-4

"Jesus said to him, 'You must love the Lord your God with all your heart, with all your soul, and with all your mind. This is the greatest and the first commandment.

The second resembles it: You must love your neighbour as yourself." Mt. 22: 37-39

Love:

"And though I have the power of prophecy, to penetrate all mysteries and knowledge, and though I have all the faith necessary to move mountains -- if I am without love, I am nothing." 1Cor. 13:2

Children:

"Parents, do not irritate your children or they will lose heart." Col. 3:21

"But when Jesus saw this he was indignant and said to them, 'Let the little children come to me; do not stop them; for it is to such as these that the kingdom of God belongs'." Mk. 10:14

Wife:

"Husbands should love their wives, just as Christ loved the Church and sacrificed himself for her." Eph. 5:25

Gratitude:

"Indeed he is not far from any of us, since it is in him that we live, and move, and exist," Acts. 17: 27c-28a

"As the chosen of God, then, the holy people whom he loves, you are to be clothed in heartfelt compassion, in generosity and humility, gentleness and patience. Always be thankful." Col. 3: 12 & 15c

"For Yahweh God is a rampart and shield, he gives grace and glory; Yahweh refuses nothing good to those whose life is blameless." Ps. 84:11

Failure:

"Let him kill me if he will; I have no other hope." Job. 13:15ab

"I know how to live modestly, and I know how to live luxuriously too: in every way now I have mastered the secret of all conditions: full stomach and empty stomach, plenty and poverty. There is nothing I cannot do in the One who strengthens me." Phil. 4: 12-13

"They keep saying, 'Our bones are dry, our hope has gone; we are done for.' So, prophesy. Say to them, "The Lord Yahweh says this: I am now going to open your graves; I shall raise you from your graves, my people, and lead you back to the soil of Israel. And you will know that I am Yahweh, when I open your graves and raise you from your graves, my people, and put my spirit in you, and you revive, and I resettle you on your own soil." Ez. 37: 11b-14a

Achievement:

"I have glorified you on earth by finishing the work that you gave me to do." John 17:4

"As a body without a spirit is dead, so is faith without deeds." Jas. 2:26

Wealth:

"Yahweh your God will make you prosper in all your labours, in the offspring of your body, in the yield of your cattle and in the yield of your soil. For once again Yahweh will delight in your prosperity as he used to take delight in the prosperity of your ancestors."
Deut 30:9

"Jesus looked round and said to his disciples, 'How hard it is for those who have riches to enter the kingdom of God!' The disciples were astounded by these words, but Jesus insisted, 'My children,' he said to them, 'how hard it is to enter the kingdom of God! It is easier for a camel to pass through the eye of a needle than for someone rich to enter the kingdom of God.' Jesus gazed at them and said, 'By human resources it is impossible, but not for God: because for God everything is possible.'" Mk. 10: 23-25, 27

"However much wealth may multiply, do not set your heart on it." Ps. 62:10b

Giving:

"Water puts out a blazing fire, almsgiving expiates sins." Ecclus. 3:30

Motivation:

"A worker's appetite works on his behalf, for his hunger urges him on." Prov. 16:26

Following my friends' examples:

"Then Jesus said to his disciples, 'If anyone wants to be a follower of mine, let him renounce himself and take up his cross and follow me." Mt. 16:24

Being present:

"As a dog returns to its vomit, so a fool reverts to his folly." Prov. 26:11

"Well, now is the real time of favour, now the day of salvation is here." 2Cor. 6: 2c

Self-examination:

"The word of God is something alive and active: it cuts more incisively than any two-edged sword: it can seek out the place where soul is divided from spirit, or joints from marrow; it can pass judgment on secret emotions and thoughts." Heb. 4:12

Language:

"From the fruit of the mouth is a stomach filled, it is the yield of the lips that gives contentment. Death and life are in the gift of the tongue, those who indulge it must eat the fruit it yields." Prov. 18: 20-21

"Hard work always yields its profit, idle talk brings only want." Prov. 14:23

"All you need say is 'Yes' if you mean yes, 'No' if you mean no; anything more than this comes from the Evil One." Mt. 5:37

Persistence:

"And Jacob was left alone. Then someone wrestled with him until daybreak who, seeing that he could not master him, struck him on the hip socket, and Jacob's hip was dislocated as he wrestled with him. He said, 'Let me go, for day is breaking.' Jacob replied, 'I will not let you go unless you bless me.'" Gen. 32: 25-27

"As for the part in the rich soil, this is people with a noble and generous heart who have heard the word and take it to themselves and yield a harvest through their perseverance." Lk. 8:15

The measurable results of my personal mission statement

A word of explanation: "before" means my life before the creation of my personal mission statement in November 2012; "after" shows the state of my life in September 2013. Since then, it has only gotten better ;)

Achievement

Before: Game logs on a Civ IV English forum, about 2 per month. Several posts per month on the card game forum

After: I started two blogs in two different communities. I've written about 140,000 words since the middle of December, including this book.

Language

Before: I didn't wonder about my speaking manners at all.

After: I am more careful in my speaking manners. I praise more; I swear less. Much less, in fact. I catch myself about twice a day when I want to say something not very wise or cruel and keep my mouth shut.

Gratitude

Before: I had a gratitude diary about my wife (started in September 2012). I occasionally had been thanking God for His blessings.

After: I started two additional gratitude diaries. One about my kids, where I write at least three positive things about each of them every day. In the other one, I write about 10 things I am grateful for in every day I live.

Giving

Before: I gave to charities about 2 percent of my income.

After: I gave to charities 3.85 percent of my income on average.

Wealth

Before: I saved about 4.5 percent of my income.

After: I saved 20.8 percent of my income on average. My savings doubled from October 2012 to May 2013.

Self examination

Before: I thought about my life once, maybe twice, per year.

After: Since the beginning of May 2013, I do self-analysis on a daily basis. I have about 150 pages of notes from those sessions. Before May, I did it irregularly - about once, twice per week.

Failure

Before: Each failure was devastating for me, so I tried very hard to do nothing - it's the only way to not fail at all.

After: The failures are still hurting me a lot, but I try to find a good side in each. I learn from my mistakes. I do what I have to do, anyway.

I notice progress in other areas as well, but they are more spiritual and hard to describe in specific, measurable terms.

Oh, and in March 2014, I changed *"I'm becoming a writer"* into *"I am a writer."*

Free Gift for You

Thanks for reading all the way to the end. If you made it this far, you must have liked it!

I really appreciate having people all over the world take interest in the thoughts, ideas, research, and words that I share in my books. I appreciate it so much that I invite you to visit: www.michalzone.com, where you can register to receive all of my future releases absolutely free.

You won't receive any annoying emails or product offers or anything distasteful by being subscribed to my mailing list. This is purely an invite to receive my future book releases for free as a way of saying thanks to you for taking a sincere interest in my work.

Once again, that's www.michalzone.com

A Favor Please

I used to actively discourage my readers from giving me a review immediately after they read my book. I asked you for a review only once you began seeing results. This approach was against common sense and standard practice. Reviews are crucial for a book's visibility on Amazon. And my approach severely hindered me from getting my message out to people just like you, who stand to benefit from it.

I was convinced about that when "Master Your Time in 10 Minutes a Day" became a best-seller. Essentially, I've gotten a number of reviews in a short amount of time, but most of those reviews were the 'plastic' ones we all dislike on Amazon: "Great book! Great content! Great reading! Great entertainment!" Such reviews simply don't carry much weight; anybody could leave a review like that without even reading the book.

In the end, it didn't matter, and my book skyrocketed up the best-seller ranks, anyway. More people than ever have had the chance to get my book in their hands. I'm grateful for this, because more people have received the means to take control over their time and their destiny.

I want to ask a favor of you. If you have found value in this book, please take a moment and share your opinion with the world. Just let me know what you learned and how it affected you in a positive way. Your reviews help me to positively change the lives of others. Thank you!

Resources

According to my promise, please find below some nuggets of personal mission statement examples.

First of all, I warn you against all kind of generators and templates on the Web. If you want to have a personal mission statement, you need to pour your soul into it, and no kind of tool will help you do that. Templates limit your creativity. The final product you get is always less than you could do by yourself.

The Internet is full of "good advice" regarding the creation of a personal mission statement, but good quality examples are few and far between. I stopped searching on subsequent pages the moment I found in someone's ruminations why didn't he write his mission statement. The search results I included have one big advantage over the rest: they are authentic, original and personal.

http://www.franklincovey.com/msb/inspired/mission statement examples - a few famous people's examples. And the only personal mission statement generator I can recommend. And even its results, you should treat as a sample and not the final product. (Unless you precisely know your mission and you are able to state it within an hour - just like Wally Amos).

http://examples.yourdictionary.com/examples/exampl
es-of-mission-statements.html - at the bottom of the
page, you will find several neatly-chiseled sentences for
a personal mission statement

http://www.inspirational-sayings-in-
action.com/example-of-a-personal-mission-
statement.html - several good examples and a few good
tips. The only critical remark I have is that most of
them are written in the future tense.

http://www.cvtips.com/career-choice/career-
statement-and-personal-mission-examples.html - a few
examples. A little too short but *lege artis* - present tense,
positive, etc.

http://www.thechangeblog.com/how-a-personal-
mission-statement-can-help-you-change/ - a nice
example in the future tense, plus a few tips

Recommended additional lectures:

"The 7 Habits of the Highly Effective People" by
Stephen R. Covey

"Man's Search for Meaning" by Viktor E. Frankl

"Think and Grow Rich" by Napoleon Hill

About the Author

I'm Michal Stawicki and I live in Poland, Europe. I've been married for over 15 years and am the father of two boys and one girl. I work full time in the IT industry, and recently, I've become an author. My passions are transparency, integrity and progress.

In August 2012, I read a book called "The Slight Edge" by Jeff Olson. It took me a whole month to start implementing ideas from this book. That led me to reading numerous other books on personal development, some effective, some not so much. I took a look at myself and decided this was one person who could surely use some development.

In November of 2012, I created my personal mission statement; I consider it the real starting point of my progress. Over several months time, I applied several self-help concepts and started building inspiring results: I lost some weight, greatly increased my savings, built new skills and got rid of bad habits while developing better ones.

I'm very pragmatic, a "down to earth" person. I favor utilitarian, bottom-line results over pure artistry. Despite the ridiculous language, however, I found there is value in the "hokey-pokey visualization" stuff and I now see it as my mission to share what I have learned.

My books are not abstract. I avoid going mystical as much as possible. I don't believe that pure theory is what we need in order to change our lives; the Internet age has proven this quite clearly. What you will find in my books are:

- detailed techniques and methods describing how you can improve your skills and drive results in specific areas of your life
- real life examples
- personal stories

So, whether you are completely new to personal development or have been crazy about the Law of Attraction for years, if you are looking for concrete strategies, you will find them in my books. My writing shows that I am a relatable, ordinary guy and not some ivory tower guru.